Joy of Cocaine and Addiction Recovery

The Surrender and Resurrection of The Soul

By

Carlton 'Moore' Robinson

authorHOUSE

1663 LIBERTY DRIVE, SUITE 200
BLOOMINGTON, INDIANA 47403
(800) 839-8640
www.authorhouse.com

First published by AuthorHouse 06/22/04

ISBN: 1-4184-5445-1 (e)
ISBN: 1-4184-5444-3 (sc)

Printed in the United States of America
Bloomington, Indiana

This book is printed on acid-free paper.

Dedicated to the memories of lifelong friends, schoolmates and neighbors Kiethco "Kiki" Wright and Wayde "Mulled" Poitier

Kiki visited me on the morning that he died asking that I accompany him to 'taboo' drug counseling meeting. Content at home with a few rocks while still denying my drug problem I refused his offer. He passed through a few times that day in wild frenzy. That night I got the call that he was found hanging in his closet.

To Mulled, while recovering himself ventured beyond the edge to rescue me during my last use of cocaine April 23rd., 1985. Sadly, he returned to the drug world unable to shake its comfort zone. His lifelong aspiration was to become an actor and walk in the footsteps of his uncle, Sir Sydney Poitier.

TABLE OF CONTENTS

FORWARD

JOY OF COCAINE RECOVERY: SURRENDER AND RESSURECTION OF THE SOUL

This book is valuable and different in that the author's inner perspectives explore some of the personal, internal battles and issues the addict faces during the surrender to addiction then recovery. It is important to know that an active addict or one going through recovery interprets his newfound horizons in unique ways as addiction to cocaine opens up strange new worlds.

That a person who has earned or possesses all the trappings of success can allow cocaine to seemingly unconscionably bring on ravages of degradation to his life is phenomenal. The slide into hell with cocaine counters everything precious and known to us. For an individual to escape the forces of cocaine addiction calls for an understanding of that roadmap in order for him to stand a chance at recovery, especially that the greatest enemy lies within the mind.

Some issues discussed here pertinent to a recovering addict are: links between mind, body and soul; regaining life's lost values; pleasure and depression levels of cocaine; making the mind master the crucial moments of pre-determination.

This writer has surrendered then resurrected from the ravages of cocaine addiction going on nineteen years. He has recounted that secret inner-battle and war. Recovering cocaine addicts do at times feel possessed, invaded and being controlled. The addict must understand that years or months free from the drug may only be an innocent deception, as the battle to overcome it may take years of practicing a healthy lifestyle. Having awareness of the pitfalls of recovery may help addicts defy the high failure rate.

To rehabilitate and resurrect oneself from cocaine is a time of challenge and internal wars as denial of cocaine's ultra-orgasmic pleasure requires superhuman mystical, emotional, spiritual and physical strength developments of their own. The pleasurable consequences of addiction seem to suppress, overcome then swallow the meaning of life itself.

With millions worldwide addicted to cocaine, and praying for a way to salvage their infected lives, this book could present a glimmer of inspiration for the hopeless. In many cases of cocaine addiction, all the addict needs is a direction toward possible cure, and then a fire of recovery begins to ignite.

Cocaine addiction creates inner conflicts of every kind between the pre-addict, the addict and the recovering addict. Recovery then too must bring one to greater understanding of a myriad of conflicts the new tri-person is presented with: the old self, the addict and the recovering addict.

Within the active addict's mind a conscious battle rages as the pre-addict's personality constantly feels betrayed by the active addict and his now alien behavioral drug induced destructive exploits. Smeagol from Lord of The Rings is a perfect example of the confusion and inner betrayal of loyalty.

An inner battle rages as the old conscience is made to confront acts committed by the rewired being. The pre-addiction, old-self takes back seat and could do no more than watch the show of decay to one's self go on. However, the day arrives when the pre-addict will attempt to regain past glory then put the active addict behind, which results in the creation of a super self, one that has danced with the devil then survived to talk about it.

Sadly, the addiction to cocaine is realized only after the user surrenders so much of the self that he becomes a new person. This surrendering comes in the form of total disregard for all lifelong norms until a huge gap is created between the pre-addict and the addict. To the addict the surrendering looms subtle but ever so destructive. An observer would notice the addict's clash of personalities and complete abandonment of the established emotional, physical and cultural norms of life.

The human, driven by the most ancient of instincts – gratification stimulation through pleasure – the active addict is compelled to succumb and surrender in barges of desperation that in essence creates a rewired totally new being.

Cocaine greatly exceeds the pleasure threshold designed into man. This ultra orgasmic traumatic experience creates a new geneses to the soul, one which begs with wonder and awe in a new and unknown universe that transcends then abandons the old human pleasure gratification points.

The addict – the resulting new person – does not consider the discarded past norms as something missed, rather, relishes solely in the desperations to seek more of this new ultra orgasmic delight. In a short time this delight alone becomes the sole apex of existence then in the end existence itself.

Recovery is made possible by the irreconcilable conflicts and agitations generated by cocaine that desecrates and rewires the mind, body and soul of the user. These self-inflicted wounds must be healed. After all, life goes on.

This book will attempt to take the reader into the responses of addiction and recovery that may give hope and a new inner understanding of what it takes to fight a great battle to resurrect the body, mind and soul through over coming cocaine addiction.

CHAPTER 1

BODY SPIRIT MIND SOUL.

Ancient South Americans regarded the coca leaf as the food of the gods. It linked the body, mind and spirits as one then used the purified soul to journey to the heavens. Ancient medicine contained in the leaf allowed man to talk with time and each spirit and soul connected with destiny.

The leaf enabled chosen spiritualists or Caciques to read the awareness of other's thoughts and of destiny connect through spiritual and bodily channels the mind, body, soul, time and beyond.

The paranormal and supernatural could be seen as part of life's order, or just simply mere fantasy and outside our grasp and control. We are all familiar with circumstances and outcomes which may lead some to believe in awareness's beyond the five senses. Cocaine maybe, opens wide that gate of linkage between what we see through our physical eyes and our spiritual eyes, both are realized through one awareness, one brain.

All cocaine addicts know of extensions of awareness beyond the normal. Somehow cocaine is the magical key to gates between the body and soul. Many persons attract spirits of a mix of both good and evil. With our extended awareness beyond the five human senses, or by virtue of the addict being opened to another world where maybe other entities can peer within our souls, spirits, minds and material world makes cocaine the gateway of the gods.

The scope of cocaine's rewiring the depth and tolerance threshold of our sensuous, nervous and electrical systems extend

1

into all dimensions including the spiritual. It becomes natural for addicts to conduct life seeming insulated from human passion and goodwill, but as a soulless, conscienceless inhumane creature. One cannot deny that cocaine only influences the physical of life without also impacting the spiritual; after all we are creatures with foresight, intuition, present destiny and hindsight.

To venture as we addicts inadvertently did into dimensions beyond – while being vulnerable to paranormal spiritual threats of good, evil and all in between was dangerous.

While high, the greatest fears of human conscience betrayed reality. Unexplained paranormal illusions, awareness's and sounds hounded and magnified the crossroads of the then present reality where the mix of the real, imagined or unexplained existed.

Moreover, that a couple could meet as a result of a distant stare through a crowd that penetrates the soul – a hooking love at first glance effect that cements and radiates lust, surety and fulfillment begs one to question the paranormal. The staring attack-like-focus of someone upon our being with the explosive invisible connection, that lets each other's mind know, "Yes," proves that psychic forces exist. Cocaine magnifies the paranormal sensitivities.

Devastated by cocaine our bodies laid bare, helpless and weak yet an invisible strength sustains the soul and feeds it hope as if all else is lost and we surrender it all up to God. That spiritually helpless, grieving and naked feeling when we give it all up, then some invisible strength brings sustenance. God? Spirituality? A strong enough force that saves us then gives direction and strength toward awareness that spiritual forces do exist. It comes once in a lifetime, but so too the awareness extension cocaine gives to paranormal sensory reality.

The danger of cocaine lies not only in what it does to the body but what it does to the spirits of man, his soul, and those of other entities beyond. Any who venture the path of life that masters the denial to pleasure will come to master the spirits, so too those who have cried out in the soul for help against powers too strong for the will to overcome. All know of the Biblical and miraculous, invisible strengths that rescue the weak and defeated.

The life of Jesus Christ exemplifies the ultimate master of denial to the flesh, pain and pleasure. Devout priests too know the strength of the spirit through denial of the body. Rebirth in denial of the pleasures of life is the ultimate destiny and spiritual strength of the recovering addict. There is life and rebirth after the thrills to

2

the flesh brought on by cocaine. The resulting pains brought on by denying the flesh the ultimate in pleasures that cocaine delivers calls for extra human strength.

Conquer cocaine, the explorations of the spirit and soul then the thrills to the flesh will find rebirth and real joys of life. Know that recovery is a destiny painful to the body and mind. It is a journey of strength that will eventually bring victory to the spirit, mind, body and soul.

To close the gates that join the awakened flesh to cocaine's pleasure with the awakened spirits calls for extra human feats and a duty of 'clean crazy' few may journey successfully. Priests have to deny human weaknesses. If you dare ask one about challenges to the spirit, of good and of evil.

To climb the steep, painful mountain of time and success with ten tons of pleasure on your back is a journey where you are destined to encounter the strength of God. The humility of blind faith in the face of failure as the desires of the body, flesh, spirits and mind all conspire to make life itself one of horrendous sub-consequences invites the need for a higher power.

CHAPTER 2

RECOVERY GRAPH FROM DAY 1, TO 6 YEARS. IDENTIFY YOUR PHASE

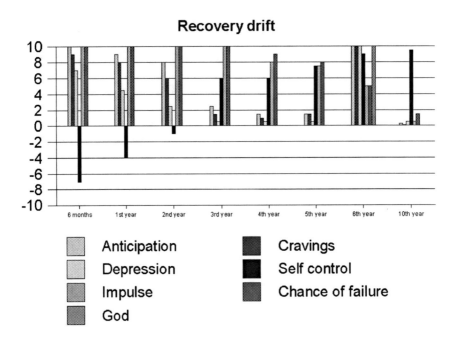

Recovery drift

Anticipation   Cravings
Depression   Self control
Impulse   Chance of failure
God

Explanations of graph

(1) Resurrecting the soul from the surrender to cocaine to 1st year.

a. Anticipation level of cocaine remains at 100%. The thrill brought on by the thought prompts toward using cocaine dominates overwhelmingly. Anticipation thrills for cocaine remain the most mentally and emotionally distractive provocation to recovery. The expectations of a hit carries greater thrill and supercedes the pleasurable physical high impact by quite a few notches, also, it can never be attained by the actual high. Anticipation is the greatest betrayer.

Up to this time in recovery, the hard wiring of the Central Nervous System (CNS) to enslaving extremes of traumatic pleasure brought on by cocaine prevents other emotional normalcy from taking root.

To counter acute anticipation or to block this excessive urge boost phase calls for almost complete ability to shut down the mind then block the train of provocative harmful thoughts. This calls for absolute mental surveillance and sensitivity to spontaneous and damaging thought prompts.

Your mind must operate like a computer's virus protector and firewall that checks all incoming and outgoing prompts. This calls for the development of an automatic, internal feedback filtering system - biofeedback.

Internal and external stimulations trigger allow spontaneous, runaway anticipation to follow through, raze havoc, then have damaging effects on any desire for healthy progress and growth away from cocaine. Only maintenance of the still within the eye of the storm can counter the damaging thoughts that spike into the calm.

The still can be described as yogic in nature or controlling a pulsating biofeedback. The triggers come in the form of normal cravings but sometimes they are subtle and as slight as a stray thought that could lead to a dangerous memory prompt or activation to use. Know which thoughts - though seeming innocent - will reach into this unwanted danger zone of stray memories that lead one to crave. Stray memories can bloom into negative desires, then ultimately cravings and use.

b. DEPRESSION

5

Having been exposed to the cocaine high with the thrill of anticipation, just everyday norms can have the seeming effect of the lows or depression. The emotional system becomes immune to the everyday passions, joys, and downs. This rewiring of the CNS by cocaine to crave for extremes beyond the everyday passions, joys and downs gives the false expectations and impression that normalcy is the dumps.

This depression in itself tries to prompt the addict to seek then force dangerous but risky joyous ups. This pit of agony likened to a tunnel of emotionally blinding dark clouds gets easier to bare within time, however these lows for the recovering addict become a state of fact and life for sometime to come.

Within the first six months many will pretend to enjoy the ecstasy of life but it may be no more than a pretentious mask of death, as a state of depression can only be beaten by naturally weaning yourself from the highs of cocaine through time or determination, and will power. Time remains the ultimate healer of this kind of depression or withdrawal.

c. CRAVINGS nag acute and severe within the first six months of recovery. Small objects that resemble the white of cocaine prompt the anticipation phase and possible runaway thoughts. The scent of cigarette smoke, drug conversations, matches or any portable source of fire, pipes or basic cocaine paraphernalia begin a mental trail that will end in severe cravings.

d. IMPULSE that can result in lose to mental control then automatic use within a whim of rage that binds the mind registers at a hard knock 100%. Sobriety is unstable.

With most of our being at this time geared toward the will to use, it is to the addict's interest to be confined within a controlled environment. You lose it when body, will, mind, emotions and soul become overcome, blinded and paralyzed by a spike in anticipation and desire to use. Impulses, although overwhelming lasts for moments that can seem an unbreakable eternity. Our cocaine induced rewired control mechanism takes hold then grips the person.

Self control with prayers, and the ability to master the still to the point of ceasing negative prompts then directing healthy thoughts at will can undermine impulse.

e. CHANCE OF FAILURE remains high at 100%. Taking into consideration that the reconstituted addict has not short circuited the cocaine hardwiring to his CNS and countered cocaine induced thoughts with overpowering positive reinforcements, dreams and hope.

f. SELF CONTROL varies depending on whether the addict is in a rehabilitation setting or in open society. Lack of self-control within a controlled environment limits the addict going out of control then leaving the sanctuary. In the freedom of society lack of self-control could be a mere thought away.

(2) 1ᴿᴰ TO 2ᴺᴰ YEAR.

Considering that up to the first year of recovery no aspect is taken for granted, success should remain on course. Follow-ups, the close contact with rehabilitation councilors, having understanding spousal or family members, and the sponsor official, all encourage success and sobriety.

This sponsor becomes the do-or-die rescue person when all hell breaks lose and the addict ends up in peril, failure and acute depression.

a. ANTICIPATION and susceptibility to it remains high but is relative to the amount of counter measures practiced. Having survived up to a year sober proves that the addict is working the rehabilitation program. The addict at this time must have strained at survival then progressed to levels of personal achievements, though with the urge to use at high levels of alluring gratification.

The thrill recollection of cocaine high could be incessant, along with the prompts toward using. If the rehabilitation program was worked as demanded by councilors, though attacked by anticipation, systems in place should bring and maintain success.

Like phantom nightmares anticipation haunts, as the need for the cocaine thrill emotionally dampens real achievement. The ultra high gratifying promise of cocaine makes anticipation a real battle to overcome.

Levels of internal counter measures, mind control, sub-audible moaning or ceasing to breath at the moment of cocaine-related-thought-detection tend to block the runaway trains of thought.

b. **DEPRESSION** is lessoned as degrees of joys and appreciations rise to near pre-addiction internal and external gratifications that once gave wholesome joys. The phantom echoes of addiction that created degraded levels of conscience and emotions, and grown immune so as to facilitate cocaine and its despicable deeds taunt to be reawakened.

c. **CRAVINGS** remain high as memory bombardments and sights of cocaine paraphernalia can lead to desires to use. The successful recovering addict should be most confident at this time that time takes care of cravings. However the urges to use become stronger. Care must be taken, and risks should be avoided.

d. **IMPULSE** to use remain at 100% and just a thought away. The break down of any of the safety parameters that encircle the addict, or a lapse in thought control will lead to an out of control situation.

e. **CHANCE OF FAILURE** remains at 100%.

f. **SELF CONTROL** will show improvements as a result of mastering and having respect for who, what, where, as regards the addicts physical and emotional environment.

FOLLOW UP TREATMENT remains a must so as to gauge our standards in comparison to those who have succeeded before us and walked the walk of failure or success.

(3) 2ND TO 3RD YEAR.

Hormones rage to test the world on all your own wings. There is light at the end of the clouded tunnel at this point, so too are hidden dangers for the best and most determined.

a. **ANTICIPATION** - jolts of ecstatic expectations that precipitate a craving along with being vulnerable to them dominate. The frequency and degree of anticipation lessens.

b. **DEPRESSION** grows almost to near sustainable normalcy as the feelings of agitation, anguish and irritability become overcome by pre-addictive joys and appreciations.

c. **CRAVINGS** are lowered, but stimulations to the sight of paraphernalia, dreams, cocaine inspiring and related conversations could be deadly serious.

d. **IMPULSE** remains high as life must remain guarded, with a suspicious state of mind. Care must still be taken to unforeseen dangers. Plans should be in place to take evasive actions to the inevitable. You should have practiced survival maneuvers to counter encounters by undesirable situations.

e. **CHANCE OF FAILURE** remains at 100% as the addict still stands a great chance of taking risks or behaving out side counseling specifications.

f. **SELF CONTROL** is on hand as the desires to survive prevail to take on momentums of their own. This natural drive inspires its own energy through doing the right thing.
Survival becomes a reward of its own. The joys of 'just life itself' lives as a vital stimulation of its own.

(4) 3RD TO 4TH YEAR. The caterpillar has wings but must keep bridges intact.

The third year of recovery you could embrace the fresh air as a feel of genuine independence surges. You have a mastery of internal and external environments, your firm yes and your no toward smiling deceptions. Fear of cocaine is now gone and so a new dangerous phase begins. [This is the year of greatest possible stupidity.]

a. **ANTICIPATION** has a lessoned effect almost to the point of immunity in that pleasurable surges stop popping up that once drove and compelled a hit. Drug related memories have a negative

9

effect now. Cross currents are produced as maybe for the first time now, cocaine produces a desired bad and negative taste to the conscience. Memories of cocaine days are filtered more clearly now and are seen as definitely undesirable regardless of the uncontrollable and ravaging pleasure it delivered. Strange curiosities develop in the form of the innocent deception.

Clear memories hold of a simple, little white rock. The mind beckons for understanding then challenges itself that such a small white thing could really do damage. This is the period of greatest failure to recovering addicts. Many fall at this point. This is the breaking point every addict must pass. That the fear factor of cocaine is gone the open mind must consciously walk away from it. Over the years cocaine was a chance occurrence that always existed but shunned out of fear. There are no longer the automatic sense of fears as a buffer. It is up to you now. You must determine whether to walk forward or backward.

b. DEPRESSION is all but non-existent and reflects more that of normal ups and downs.

c. CRAVINGS are unusual and seeming innocent.

d. IMPULSE remains guarded, as you must execute conscious well thought out choices and decisions toward the environment one chooses to survive within. This is a mentally foggy period. The addict must foresee the type of situations that would lead him toward an emergency and bring him to the point of calling for help. Situations grow similar to control of the moment, but this time you have hours or days to see danger then to reflect. The addict must know when to reach for help. A conscious wholesome person should have developed at this point with the foresight to keep on living and out of danger. Many get an adrenaline rush from taking risks. You are near to being the very person that got you into problems in the first place, a very dangerous person.

e. CHANCE OF FAILURE remains high but lessened as an automatic event as innocent deceptions along with newly found confidence could lead to fatal risk taking. Fear of cocaine becomes diminished. This is the year of greatest failure for addicts. Carefree, daring, silly, chancy, insecurities, confusion and curiosities come to the forefront which lead the addict to doubt and question whether **'cocaine really was that dangerous'**, beckons.

Somehow within the mental mixing zone a separation takes place between memories, conscience, ego and self confidence as humility is forgotten so too the fear of cocaine. At times as these, humility is the greatest strength. Remaining humble to, and respecting progress is an outmost, as **'if life is not broken do not attempt to fix it.'**

At a smiling and confidant state of assurance, now is the time to take complete control of all future actions, impulses then mentally anticipate possible dangerous contacts and safe reactions.

Active addicts may recognize your success then reach out – fine. But the recovering addict should never venture into crack houses to rescue the afflicted as I know many that have failed in this risky venture including the person who rescued me, Wayde 'Mulled' Poitier, now deceased, nephew of internationally acclaimed actor Sir Sydney Poitier.

f. SELF CONTROL is challenged but the development of thinking, rewired conscience should save the day. Cocaine should now mean a matter of right and wrong. Self-control should have now been exceeded to the highest point known to the addict. Success is more in sight; also, a feeling of well being is experienced. Life could bubble with joy and exuberance.

(5) 4TH TO 5TH YEARS & 5th to 6th.

With the exception of self-control, which progresses along with appreciation for life's common value and progress all remain good. The rewiring to pre-addict values should be well cast within your system.

d. IMPULSE must remain as guarded. Trusting and letting friends into your life should be monitored and remember that at all times sobriety comes first. For most addicts close contact with individuals whom we trusted got us into trouble, therefore, trust of acquaintances should be kept as guarded for safety precautions.

e. CHANCE OF FAILURE decreases with genuine appreciation of values for the good progresses in life. Once it works stick with it. Success falls into place.

YEAR 6. Nightmares from hell.

This could be the most dangerous year of them all. Also it will be the year you could genuinely find God.

Cocaine fires its final volley of blows from hell. You are knocked to your back then all imaginings of what could go wrong manifests themselves. You are struck with failures to your mind, body soul and seemingly invaded by every evil spirit conceivable. All within a blinding scoop of time that relentlessly twirls you in a whirlwind of absolute failure to all that you accomplished for an eternal lifetime of hard work, progress, joy and achievement.

You are betrayed from within mixed with all your external surroundings as they become one. Fantasy and reality take you on a ride to hell. Have you ever dreamt that you were falling from the sky or into a deep hole, and then you awaken, jump from bed with your heart racing in fear as you gasp the surreal imminence of death? The ultimate in fear and terror scourers your body and mind leaving you with a near heart attack, emotionally drained, and a body enveloped and dripping in cold sweat.

As in a twilight state, images grip and emotions betray. You would bitterly kill yourself in denial that you just used. You cry in disbelief, yet the fantasy of use seems surreal. You could feel the high pulsating through your veins, the pleasure roaming your toes, fingertips, groan, as your body bathe in cocaine's pleasurable bliss.

"More, more," begs tantalizingly and insistently. The craving for the next hit drives you to locate your money as your mind merges with known latent surveillance of where the pusher men peddle their illicit drugs from.

But no! Certain elements seem out of place. You question, "Where is the table with crack and cigarette you just used from? Where are the matches? Where are your basing friends you just used with?"

You notice the still and quiet of reality, except your body sweats profusely to the floor. Your heart pounds with the excitability that you just took a hit. Your body trembles for the next hit and recoils from the last.

You grip your money, look to the door then plead, "God no please. Dear God no save me."

Something drops you to your knees and you continue to pray for strength not to exit that front door with your money on your way to the pusher man. Your body trembles. You feel invaded by spirits and out of control of your will.

You scream to God, "No." Visions hold firm within the pictures of the mind letting you know the exact whereabouts of the pusher man and your money.

Urges skyrocket out of control and out of your world of belief, however it all seems super real. Your body is sweating profusely. You seem to have probably took a hit and it is relived as one of the greatest ever. You long for more. You ache for more. It was just like a mighty, single moment of time just passed since you last used. Your cocaine wires are back to their full strength and reality. Normalcy has been thrown to hell.

Your senses suddenly awaken to a new reality, that of the old addict you were six years ago, and it is you all over again. The past years of success become compressed into a forgettable dot of time. The demand to hit is 100% active.

a. Anticipation jumps over 100%.

c.   Cravings ache your body. Your mind focuses solely on the anticipation of the hit that longs to come seeming from beyond heaven.

Your hold of cash burns for cocaine. The pusher man beckons in you from your latent avoidance intelligence as subconscious knowledge of his whereabouts. It is just - all go - now. Again, six years is painful success and growth becomes compressed into a single blink of irrelevant moment in time.

> **d.   IMPULSE** pains and fires with certainty to break free. Your body stenches and your mind searches for surety that beyond all reasonable doubt, you just used and you need more immediately.

e. CHANCE OF FAILURE remains as low. The accomplishment of you moving on to use cocaine fights against God as strength in time of need, all you achieved, trust, confidence, and the loved ones in your life.

The nightmare is all over within five minutes, however you are terrified now. No more taking things for granted. There is a new respect for cocaine. The small values like life-itself are again gratified.

For days though, all things white and small become a threat. Emotionally, you are back at square one. You fight to regain self-confidence. You reach for your still, that quiet pulse that is as hard as steel and backed by God. You come to realize you are now a part of everyday life with its ups and downs. Only, you now have a special phantom. One you have probably seen for the last time at this magnitude. But you know he is there.

f. Self control strains to let go. You sweat the fight. You must muster the strength to handcuff your body, now out of control as the old stranger has returned. You know him well.   Your hands tremble. Your mind is back to active addiction state.

Is it real or not? You are not sure. Everything is in place – except; where is the smoke, the pipe, the matches. You cry for it to be a simple nightmare. Ashamed, you dare not talk to your sponsor or one emotionally closest to you. After all, you were supposed to be free.

Finally, you question the impulsive determination then reassure yourself that, "This is not me."

A massive betrayal and illusion took place that resulted in all things small and white once again, as six years prior, the enemy, so too money. You search for inner honesty, only what do you say?

You realize your limitations then acknowledge that which you vehemently denied, that surely you would always be a recovering addict. Relaxations and confidence return cocaine to the enemy, but now at a greater level because you realize you have come too far to fall back now. Cocaine is a threat to all things deemed valuable: emotional, material, financial, spiritual or fanciful.

You shiver from fear at this dream that enveloped body, mind and soul in a wrap as real as life.

CHAPTER 3

MASTERING THE MOMENT. FACING OUR INNER SMEAGOL IN LORD OF THE RINGS

"If only I had," is the cry of all recovering addicts after the fact of painful relapse can no longer be denied and the forbidden cocaine high has expended its hypnotic and tantalizing grip. That damning 'if' awareness. If -- condemns.

If reveals and admits that other possibilities and consequences existed outside of the one that led to cocaine high. Revealed is that there existed numerous choices that could have been made at a particular moment in time that could have resulted in varying numbers of consequences between life and death.

Many points of no return co-conclusions could exist within the same breath as a point of return, a time when the possibility existed to step back from a situation and its consequence. That magical determining moment, when 'if' only we could freeze our reality then watch our phantom go ahead then do the deed, sparing our conscience body and souls the outcome.

Life just does not work that way. However, moments of self control or lack of it determine destiny. We become like Smeagol from Lord Of The Rings who faces that duality of purpose. The strongest processes that can threaten self-control are the runaway thoughts that lead to spontaneous action as cocaine thoughts do mushroom to the point of exciting the body toward every eventuality to obtain it.

That moment of destiny whereby we are still in conscious control of our yes and no, when we could draw down, then still the mind must be practiced. Ways must be learnt to short-circuit to-the-point, on-time, at-hand, actionable thoughts at the point of mental creation. Then using foresight and experience you should see which thoughts are destined to be dangerously drug provocative following into the next moment.

Some recovering addicts have been heard screaming from the top of their lungs, "NO," in order to fight back then dispel oncoming bad thoughts. Oftentimes, screams could be heard while in public, as by all means the 'provocative phantom' must be dispelled.

The instant of active thoughts must be controlled at its creation. They must not be allowed to bloom into runaway mental viruses that demand cocaine use upon the will. Again, mastering the moment could only be achieved by short-circuiting the mind, body and soul by instantly ceasing the breathing rhythm momentarily at the point of thought. The chain of activation thought-prompts that lead into the desire to use cocaine must be broken.

After the chaos of potential threatening thoughts, calm always ensues.

CHAPTER 4

COLD TURKEY WINDOW TO THE SOUL

For some reason a certain character type of hardened addicts simply turn their backs on cocaine without the use of rehabilitation systems or any belief in a higher power; they just quit cold turkey.

In one single shot, they marshal body, mind and soul then depart from cocaine use. Baffled, many are left in disbelief, but time takes care of doubters and many doubters have become believers. Maybe no one knows the degree of inner contemplation and soul searching the addict goes through in silence before that final moment of decision. However, they just up and quit.

In what must be perceived as a window to the soul these persons are seemingly able to switch off their hard-wired configuration for cocaine within the blink of an eye. What depth of vision they master to execute such superpower draws the envy and curiosity of many.

But, it is this will that each addict desire to possess; that will to execute the thousands of promises of – no more – to cocaine, then walk away never to look back. What pain – if any - the cold turkey endures in silence as he turns a final back on cocaine can only be imagined.

Maybe cocaine use remained a peripheral scare fraught with mistrust from the beginning. Maybe these cold turkey people dived in while harnessed to a safety line. But somehow, they do manage to walk out of the hole and don't look back.

Addicts could only speculate becoming the personality type to dive into the dark holes without safety harnesses blind. Overconfidence is one of the vises of the addict. He always believes he could get out of any situation. Super human risk-takers faithfully take on the sweet lure of innocent deception, confident in their belief in knowing the way in and out.

However, once into the dark cave of addiction, blind and abysmal passages appear then the addict bares all inhibitions to the fruits of pleasure as he dives into rallying troughs of ever-pleasurable rewards without a harness.

The cold turkey addict who plunged into the abysses did so with one eye closed and one eye open. Guided by awareness attached to reality, the cold turkey person slips out of addiction due to his one eye open, which kept a balance between reality and the fact that cocaine is a consuming betrayer.

The cold turkey addict probably keeps his eyes on passionate dreams and desires. Feeling threats to his long-standing dreams he quickly determines that cocaine is the threat and not the savior.

The full-fledged addict in recovery has to reinvent dreams, alternatives and harness onto them although cocaine has turned them into faint illusions overcome only by determination, conviction and belief. The depths of personal conviction and belief in pursuit of dreams are the determining factors toward recovery. A hope not discarded but adhered to propels the cold turkey out of the grip of cocaine addiction.

CHAPTER 5

DESPERATION HAS NO CONSCIENCE

The demand for a cocaine high brings an addict to the point of surrendering then sacrificing life itself. The desperation for cocaine has no checkpoints and is open ended therefore the desire for cocaine most often wins over fear of harm, spiritual or social value systems. The addict will devise all manners of creativity and his ingenuity explodes to all levels of deception in order to get a cocaine high. No amount of love for person or item is spared in the desire to hit.

Hearts become broken and finances vaporize with seeming remorselessness on the part of the addict. The addict abandons material, emotional, dependents and support systems. The addict becomes a new creation as cocaine becomes his sole reason for existence. Cocaine spares no opportunity toward its preservation. The addict becomes only a tool to that end.

The addict's heart, body, emotions and soul ache toward all possible means and manner to obtain cocaine. In sad desperation, the addict would surrender a wholesome home with family, material valuables then finally the house itself to addiction.

The cold reality of destroyed purpose, lives and hope will come as a dream and the addict will ponder, although already resigned to surrender to the next inevitable lower level of desperation, "Did I do that?" - impacts with glaring surrealism, taken away from the pain of reality. In the midst of confusion, denial, acceptance comes swears of, "Never again."

After having sworn never again, you paint on the repose of firm straightforward determination. Your heart throbs in sad indignation and self pity, yet race at this new opening of opportunity. A new level of lowly success, that another cocaine high has been accomplished and realized. A new awakening is born with multiple promises.

Once challenged lower lows of desperations are conquered until the addict reaches a point where he has exhausted and surrendered his body, mind, soul and spirit to the pursuit of cocaine. In this state of inner loss and outward physical depravation the addict will meander through life an enigma and a curiosity.

As the prospects of a high reveals itself the adrenaline begins to flow, the pupils dilate, and the heart rate and breathing quicken. The mind narrows then locks. The body and soul develop a sense of dispensability. Existence itself solely focuses on the demand for a high. There can be no compromise, body, mind or soul. The spirit, that which links us to the universe becomes compromised and breached as our human being reduces to animalistic impulses.

The addict sheds any and all semblance to humanness and humanity as we invite and expose ourselves to any will or whim desired by others. Also, life itself is reduced and is seen as dispensable. To that end even another's life loses its humanness and could be bartered then sold. The prospects of desperation makes comprehensible any and all eventualities conceived unbridled in scope including the taking of human life and the loss of your own.

CHAPTER 6

FOOLS RECOVERY

A time bomb is produced most often when out of pressure an addict feels genuinely compelled to stay from drugs to prove something to himself or to others. Abstinence is illusive in the long term as the time bomb ticks without the aid of proper guidance toward rehabilitation.

Prison sentences tend to produce grand illusions to family and acquaintances who sit on the outside then think that time itself will heal addiction. This fools recovery has lead to many disappointed expectations. Time locked away for years, or months or spontaneous inner convictions may only hold back use for a while.

The acute desire for cocaine and impending relapse can remain on hold in the mental shelf for days and months within any given environment that the addict is accustomed to. Without the conviction to quit along with rehabilitation tools, relapse is almost a certainty.

At times, armed with the conviction to not use, an addict will with the best of intentions and desires make all the wrong moves. Desire alone is a single element on the road to recovery. However, the addict must make fundamental changes to his state of mind and his respect for physical environment.

To think that you could quit cocaine but change nothing within your lifestyle is setting yourself up for a relapse. An addict will easily fool himself by remaining with fellow cocaine acquaintances while withholding spending money or even sit in while they use. The temperament of the addict is important.

In fools recovery the addict could display a very happy and exuberant demeanor. The level and steady-headedness necessary to sustain sobriety is painful. The mask of euphoria only sets up impending gloom and relapse.

The recovering addict must know how to find the inner still, where neither drug related thoughts, or sightings could move the will and subdue discipline.

CHAPTER 7

FAITH GOD

Many recovering addicts use God in order to skirt the rigors and natural disciplinary course of the recovery process. Yet some surrender the circumstances of their lives to God that their will is no longer theirs to master. It is this conviction of humility, helplessness, resignation and emptiness that invites God's overwhelming healing power.

On the other hand, the belief that an addict could sit and receive individual and special treatment from God toward recovery I cannot question because the occurrence does exist. For many though the strangling urge to use cocaine is never quenched solely by prayer. On the road to recovery there could be millions of mountains to overcome within a day. Incessant calling on God's name to cushion fears, overcome cravings that stab the will, or just to motion the will forward become countless.

Any addict who contemplates recovery then executes the will toward it must take stock of the enormous powers he has to overcome. The battle for sobriety weighs as a sobering prospect due to the heavy forces and tasks ahead. That cocaine addiction involved forces beyond the mind and body and into the spiritual, calls on addicts to call on God's help to conquer those intense and controlling forces beyond our strength.

Most recovering addicts find God when there is no way out and he has used the last of his will. The genuine cry in the dark storms to still the rough seas of entombing, overwhelming and fearful cocaine peril produces miracles. God finds a way into he that calls out in peril. It becomes a journey of faith where you take a peaceful walk with Jesus. This mountain top experience brings the addict to an inner calm where he feels the still within.

The experience of the calm and still within becomes a drive force, a gauge and a place of strength, solace and solitude – an inner solid rock. The still along with sobriety are constantly threatened by cocaine memories, every day events and dreams.

When God becomes that Uplifting Faith Experience then the addict has transcended just callously trying to invoke His power. God is met in the heat of battle in the grips of despair with forces trying to take control. To see God you must fight and take on the Devil of addiction in the trenches of battle in the recesses of our threatened soul. The strength and calm grace you feel as you face the world after the mighty battle lets you know that indeed something extra powerful had taken place beyond mere human limitations.

CHAPTER 8

GENISES MODE

Crushed in body, mind, spirit and soul then squeezed into doom, the spirit must be placed in a strengthened position or enlightened condition to pull the rest of the being to recovery and acceptance of all of life. A broken spirit dooms and drowns in mire where this hopelessness stagnates recovery.

Hope is a great reserve abundant in energy. But where do we find the drive or spirit to dream of a life after, with all destroyed except life itself. Provisions that strengthen the soul come in the form of the humblest conditions of life like this moment of life and the breath we breathe.

From the cataclysmic chaos of cocaine addiction the addict must be able to find inner and outer peace. Solace comes from without and within and they either raze havoc or bring serenity to the mind and body.

By surrounding yourself with persons from your innocence as far back as kindergarten could produce a rejuvenation state on the mind. These comfort zones and comfort conditions nurture and in doing so strengthens. To be taken back to the time when life was carefree and abounding in child's play reenergizes the emotional growth state and serves as confidence and moral boosters.

A problem many have with rehabilitation is in after desiring to be drug free to produce the environment conducive to achieve sobriety. Although inner strength must be unflinching, conditions tend to add positive energy or power or to take it away.

False confidence or false strength is a killer if received from a negative environment as they could be merely a shell and easily broken leaving the addict with a drifting for a fall. Imagine receiving hope and getting the feel good feel from a fellow very active cocaine abuser or drug peddler. This type of negative hope is destructive and drifts the recovering addict back into cocaine abuse.

Clashes between the will to quit addiction and the strong desires to use is an agonizing and relentless string of events. Contact within the physical environment that then lures and entraps, inspires addiction. This is opposed to an environment that surges free and sanitized with no recollection of cocaine's street corners, base houses, and drug personalities that all can induce cravings.

The recovering addict can derive positive energies from cherished innocent laughter against the scorn of criticisms and snare-laden, guilt ridden jabs of depression. True facts, when you are known to all as the addict, the thief, the beggar, the family wrecker, the one time millionaire, the person who sold precious everything to get high; in recovery you need a break from it all, a break from being the damned.

Yet, we must know how to survive the period of being perceived as the damned then accept our fate as such. In genesis mindset we acknowledge our past as a position from which a new beginning is being launched from but a position which we will not remain at. Once that realization is acknowledged in the will and soul the energies awakened can be tasted and dares to be tested. The feel of having that intuition that "I will survive," hulks one to want to become Atlas and lift up the world, only the world is filled heavy with the mere and meager desire to survive extreme cocaine.

To resurrect the ravages of cocaine upon the conscience as we face the garbage of deeds brought about by cocaine addiction like the events we cannot stare in the mirror at, a forgiving environment may just do the trick. An environment taken away long ago maybe the ultimate regeneration medium. A time when the bounties of innocence, expectations, energy and hope prevailed; a time of youth along with the energetic personalities that existed at that time. If only we could relive that time again. To be surrounded again by that rejuvenating embrace of time, rebounding joy, explosive optimism and fearless hope are a wellspring of growth - a genesis.

One will find that the genesis environment radiates with positives and the energies of hope where persons outside of the addiction stream radiate with dreams to strive as a common powerful factor.

26

Along the road to recovery negative prompts will come from 360 degrees. A mental battleground exists that you must forge your way through with no sight of light anywhere or no straight tunnel to walk though.

Surrounded by genesis people one can feel a glimpse of pure energy free from painful memories and hurts. This momentum can be fleeting but it gives promise and hope. Sometimes that is all the addict needs, a promise of what life once felt like; a touch of old reality – a dreamtime.

Places too can become a source of refuge. Childhood playgrounds at lunchtime hold fond memories so too the personalities of shared sunny, joyful excitement. Childhood was a great time. To be surrounded by the fountain of fulfillment reenergizes the soul like the old wooded trails that strove with unending new adventurous journeys or stepping through tidal pools. For this feel, quiet or the rush, whatever our innocence grew up to know. It is important to be taken away to familiar surroundings uncontaminated by addiction.

What is invoked during Genesis mode is a sense of strength brought about by bathing or immersing the mind into a period of our past when life abounded in purity. Purity in the sense of innocence without suspicion how the world perceived and reacted to us minus the ravages of addiction. This interaction between past childhood's peers is invigorating.

To place oneself into an environment where our spirits can get a sense of innocence against the backdrop of disharmonious clash while attempting sobriety is refreshing. To this end music too can be a source of great rejuvenation. Songs from the sixties and early seventies during our early adolescent awakening are refreshing. Songs by The Carpenters, ABBA, Bob Marley, Billy Joel, The Beatles, Rod Stewart, and other soft rock ballads and melodies.

On the other hand, lyrics from the time of active addiction can become depressing and self-defeating. Sanitized environments free from the strings of addiction frees then opens the world of innocent possibilities, something the recovering addict would get an energized drive from. To offset all negatives from without and within brings one to surges of extreme desires to overcome all that was lost then to regroup, sustain and rebuild.

27

CHAPTER 9

PLEASURE AND DEPRESSION LEVELS OF COCAINE

The pleasure and abysmal levels of cocaine can be described simply as the difference between life and death. During a high rush of pleasure reaches to placid, ecstatic tranquility where it holds and the body, mind and soul begs for it to be an eternity. In a short space of time, the freefall roller coaster begins its cragged slide then needled rest as the high expends.

The lure for cocaine is like a rest upon biting needles. It will invoke the addict to dance with death for cocaine again in order to escape then reach that ecstatic plateau within shortest possible time. At times not sparing life itself, the addict's forward charge away from resting on needles, which normalcy feels like, toward a high takes him on a voyage of regretful surrender, after all, life sometimes goes on. Yes, the addict is forced to languish and bide time as he forgoes a high to earn a livelihood; he deals with co-workers, relates with family and slips through society.

People, with society, the everyday norms become the pawns and alleyways toward a high as the addict preys upon them through prostitution, honest labor or thievery. As he garners necessary funds to get high he discards the intricacies of family, friends, work and norms of life and society. The languish is over; the eternal high sequence begins. Soon, the cragged pains stab at the mind, body and soul to relive cocaine's blazing euphoria. Again the addict languishes in turmoil among the living.

At the extreme high lies a numbness where the addict cannot realize the high sensation. For those with excessive amounts of drugs or money this can become an anti climax as there is a measured duration of pleasure the body can maintain before it reaches the threshold then go oblivious to the high. Overdose then death can follow from cocaine toxicity.

On the down side for the addict, the depression levels of cocaine is strongest due to problems and the reality while pursuing and obtaining drugs. Feelings of extreme guilt then harbor and create the will and determination to die. Cocaine intoxication could change body chemistry, mental stability and bring about unknown immeasurable influences to the soul. At the other end are those who reach abysmal pits of longing and craving where the quench for cocaine desires to be met at any and all costs.

Body, mind and spirit encounter blasts of extremes beyond our human design to secure and live within the bounds social well-being. Thus the addict becomes a threat to himself and to society. Addiction takes one beyond the realms of human civility in body, spirit, emotions and soul.

The saying goes 'the higher you go the harder and deeper you fall.' On the cocaine scale that wise saying bodes true. You can neither control the high nor the downs; the addict must however ride them both then survive. There is just this thing about cocaine, it takes you up physically but also severely downs you emotionally and spiritually.

The pleasure difference that is generated between what is naturally endowed by God for us and what cocaine takes you to creates a conflict of obedience and allegiance. The pleasure and acute painful desperation caused by cocaine enslaves then takes over all God given pleasures designed for man to bear. The addict would trade off any worldly, bodily or virtue for cocaine.

Cocaine lows and highs impose the specter of dancing with death and suicide more readily than any natural God given emotional state of joy or depression.

CHAPTER 10

OVERCOMING POINTS OF SURRENDER

Just being addicted to cocaine then having spent the last of your savings enabling your addiction opens the gate of your surrender to cocaine. In the end you may have surrendered your death to cocaine, as addiction has no limits.

Points of surrender begin from a simple friendly handout to the first dollar spent. At the point of spending the first dollar your surrender to cocaine has began; you have entered the gate.

Finances, trust, material possessions, dignity, health, life, God, family, dreams, accomplishments all become compromised and gradually surrendered to addiction until the addict arrives at the base level rock bottom of them all. Corrective events do take place along the way down in any one area where the addict is failing that could rescue the rest of his being. Unchecked, all avenues of an addict's life deteriorates.

It is a long crashing process to overcome that drift of surrender then rehabilitate oneself while on that downward spiral. Degradation along family or financial matters if noticed in time then checked could pull one from the brink of surrendering it all. Oftentimes though the addict's life is left in tatters and all things of meaning mere bare threads with no solid foundation.

With cocaine in one hand and your values in the other, one stares at the balance or lack thereof, as cocaine tends to outweigh them all. If however by some miracle one holds an entity as cherished and dear to the heart and soul enough energy may be mustered to overcome the point of surrender that concerns that item. Rescued from the bowels of addiction with emphasis on value upon a particular item could be risky if the addict uses that item as a crutch of dependency and does not dig deep within for strength.

Within small communities it is more difficult for females to overcome the stigma associated with cocaine abuse then rebound.

CHAPTER 11

ANTICIPATION: COCAINE THE BETRAYER.

Cocaine high can best be described in terms of the overwhelming realization of joys and gratifications. A meal, orgasms, rewards, drinks, hugs, cries of joy or special occasions all produce a sense of gratification. While the normal course of life agitates for rewards and substances of gratification, cocaine provides the greatest of instantaneous ecstasy. Thus, cocaine fits in well with our design as humans; it is rewarding to the body by its agitation toward the release of extremes of pleasures - the ultimate, ultra orgasmic explosion.

There is a stage of addiction much higher than the physical drug itself that is so powerful it could paralyze, weaken, tremble and lock the soul in a vice. Anticipation of a high bleeds the mind, body and soul; it is a killer worst than a cocaine high. The anticipation of a high is boundless in intensity. This preliminary high is the greatest betrayer as it can never be achieved or matched in reality.

CHAPTER 12

ADMIT THAT YOU HAVE A DRUG PROBLEM.

A most difficult phenomena, as I still do not recall admitting to a drug problem. Denial? Arrogance? I really do not know.

As an active cocaine addict 1983-85, the foresight and desire did not exist in me to depart from addiction. However, time in rehabilitation cleared my mind enough to work the fourteen basic steps to recovery. I did realize that cocaine was wrong for my life and brought stagnation. I hated the thought of stagnation.

In hindsight, everyone has a unique code to exit addiction. A passion must yearn for something of meaning to that person. The answer lies in finding out that right key to the heart. Not being able to stomach a future of stagnation became my window of conflict with cocaine.

I did not know the significance of responding to the request by doctors and councilors, "Do you admit that you have a drug problem?" I was more full of reluctance to admit having a drug problem.

However, I did quit cocaine then afterward admit to a drug problem. There is no sure road that brings an addict to see the benefits of life outside cocaine. The fisherman never calls his fish stink, and if he were to, it would be a mighty bridge to cross; an eye opener in honesty, courage and conscience.

After losing your mind body and soul to cocaine then being confronted by a loved one about a drug problem the addict will question, "A problem? What problem?"

The uncontrollable urges that fester whenever a thing, person or idea arise that anticipate cocaine or the high itself is not a problem to the addict. Life is, and cocaine is, that is all that matters. With the desire for cocaine the greatest crown of existence and achievement, how can it be a problem?

When all those things that goes wrong due to addiction become of lesser value to a high, how can cocaine be a problem? The only problem is the lack of cocaine. 'Cocaine for life'; this is the mindset of the addict.

The addict denies and denies as others are in pain but not him. Even after loss of limb and health to cocaine, its lure and high survives as unconscionably blameless.

It is wishful thinking and lost hope upon an observer who desires the addict to reach a point of conscious awareness where he places value on life - as a loss or gain - then relate those values directly with cocaine abuse. To the addict there is no connection between the two as an impenetrable wall of denial exists. This wall exists seeming as lack of desire and or self-control but an addict somehow never defends cocaine yet it   prevails as a buffer to pain and understanding.

The sweet of addiction separates the point of conscious questioning that could begin the divorce from the binding cocaine marriage. This marriage will allow the addict to withstand any gloomy eventuality to his body, mind, soul or that of others.

When your life has without conscience become unquestionably unmanageable, then acceptance of loss or pain become of lesser value than the anticipatory cocaine high the addict should begin to question sobriety, but no; he will go on to stare death in the face. He only questions his sobriety when his desire for a high is consciously seen as too threatening to the self. The aware and awakened conscience is key here.

Yet, how do you force a man engaged in a sweet drowning to raise his head above water and breath? The desire for a high knows few bounds and depends on the unique nature of the addict. With addiction having no set physical, emotional, mental and spiritual boundaries for some, death becomes the last resort. However, just short of death and at the pit of rock bottom may be a boundary for most.

Some addicts stop after: having ominous or hopeful premonitions, catching a misdirected phrase of wisdom, cross a moral borderline or threshold, or situations reach the depth of a person's inner anguish. Hardly though from negative prodding and nuisance tactics, which tend to drive the addict deeper into despair, rejection and desperation.

Some well-meaning persons to an addict's life inadvertently encourage denial through ignorance of the ways of cocaine addicts. Knowledge to the ways of an addict should also mean locking down everything that could be sold. Addicts without boundaries, which all of us fall into at points of desperation without conscience would sell all things eternal and precious.

The fight to stop cocaine is an internal battle. Those caught in-between cocaine and the addict will suffer horrendously and go through much material, financial, emotional, spiritual, drastic, unpredictable and destructive shifts in life's course.

The battle to quit cocaine lies within the conscience of the addict, which may bring down a family, business, home, nation or self, then regardless, remain within boundaries of denial to the ways of cocaine, with further destruction destined to follow.

For the addict to imagine, and then place safety as an alternative to a cocaine high is a massive leap of salvation and resurrection. Yet it happens. To see what's on the other side of the high then place it as an accomplishment to die for is a marked achievement.

The wall of addiction begins to crumble when the addict acquires a view that cocaine has become a threat to his life whether the encouragement comes as a dream, a desire, or threat to possessions and loved ones. Cocaine becomes the enemy to the conscience, after however, causing every conceivable pain to the world.

It is the event, the crossing point or mixing zone that the addict hopes to arrive at, the creation of doubt and then emerging will power to depart from cocaine. Growing guilt tweaks at the conscience and creates inertia toward love of life then disdain for cocaine.

It is a great achievement for an addict to admit that there is a dark side to his life, a potential monster within. To admit means that you agree to take on a monster within. To remain blind to the monster on the other side is to keep the gates open to possession of cocaine. This mental, and physical invasion and possession by cocaine that is one entwined within, sometimes cannot be seen and is inseparable from healthy dreams and desires.

The point of separation begins when we recognize higher ideals a higher state of conscience a dream state. At a conscience level we must perceive doom or an ominous link with cocaine; a cocaine nightmare of sorts that internalizes fear to the deepest crevasse of our being.

Cocaine as a problem, with the will to free oneself from it, is realized internally at the soul and not externally. The emotional stimulus to come to a point of admittance is not reached by the decrepit physical condition of self nor shocking loss of possessions.

The point of arrival where the borderline between sanity and insanity is made consciously clear although ineffective as a working tool starts the transition to recovery. This awareness now made separate and distinguishable, one with dreams the other with pain and loss. The desire to break the automatic pulse of cocaine use then pursue dreams starts the will toward surrender to the mismanagement of our lives. The conscious realization of loss to our well-being and health is an eye opener.

The first source of awareness is that of our basic needs not being met and made irrelevant because cocaine rewires and makes us an alien to our known self. Cocaine takes precedence over and threatens the basics of health, food, security, finances, shelter and employment.

Admitting the loss of the basic necessities of life does not mean that it constitutes the admission of cocaine addiction. Living in a state of denial in order to protect and defend addiction is the first course of existence. Reflection and deep contemplation in order to muster the will to separate the rut then move on to dreams and desires enhance the push toward recovery.

To the non-addict, non-admission to problem seems like denial of the obvious. The inability to manage one's life: health, security, food, shelter and employment. The decrepit lifestyle seems enough to admit. However, addiction is psychotic. It is the mind and the physical joys of cocaine, which the addict interprets the world through.

To the addict cocaine does not cause pain but the opposite. The lack of cocaine causes pain. This crazed state at some point must be seen as such, a crazed state. The illusion of a better life precipitates the will to put cocaine behind; but this is only an illusion. This illusion must nurture from within then at a point the nagging instilled on us from family and society sinks in.

Once the addict begins to consciously question his state he is on the road to recovery.

CHAPTER 13

SURVIVING RELAPSE

Trying to regroup your body, mind and soul to normal reality after a cocaine binge calls for massive adjustments to the senses. Like an astronaut having to adjust from a space journey your whole being faces physical and mental dimensions different from those that exist while high.

The high itself exists in a cocoon of its own reality. However once you escape to normalcy the real world appears and feels as a mentally generated delusion of suspicions where shadows, sights, sounds, touches, apparitions and paranoia of every conceivable entity take hold of the mind.

Down-time with down people is uncomfortable, where the user lacks sure mental footing. The crafty addict will know how to pretend into any situation then swing into the mood of the social environment without suspicion. However, where intimate associates or friends linger, conflicts of guilt, suspicion and conscience may develop.

The addict will search for the groove of acceptance and the zone of interpersonal and socializing comfort then adjust until he gains reassurances and confidence. Coping with discomforts from profuse sweating, eyes wide open, pace which speeds out of sync and the jitters - all the addict may desire is a calm place to rest then recoup the mind and replenish the body and soul.

A time of deep reflections follow. The addict ponders his immediate fate, loss and recovery. Conscience and fate resigned, he silently ekes his way into a ritual of learnt patterns with familiar results from the normal environment, which include street life, work and home. The semblances of everyday life are trudged out while another turn for a high awaits.

After the further relapse leaves the addict down to the dumps he faces strangers and insecurities. The outside world sees a smiling face in apparent normalcy. He smiles back as it seems the right thing to do. Wounded in body, mind and spirit your soul longs for a rest and a return to the familiar. Body dehydrated, mind exhausted, emotions lost and in denial.

The crash reveals itself on the changing tides of reality as the near past meets life's long history and a conscience is created. Disbelief is agonized. Love of familiar body, emotions, spirit, values resign to the sad obvious of lost, and spent.

A night of rampage on the body, soul and emotions assault the mixing zone of fantasy, reality, temptation, and remorse.

Again your build up motivation of dream and glory toward recovery have fallen. The run on automatic as you tell yourself 'NO' but you watch where you are going, what you are about to do.

You curse yourself as you use uncontrollably. You cry as you use again. The deal done heavy grows your emotional weight: the weight of your failure, the weight of starting your rehabilitation all over again.

Depressed and in need of rescue you call the person who swore to your aid when it all falls through – and there is no way out. The councilor becomes your death and life medium. He will bring you around. He accepts your lot without criticism.

Time to explore where you went wrong.

CHAPTER 14

THE FIRST MONTH

This is a time of great courage, great defiance and great denial. Your understanding of recovery could become your greatest defense against relapse. You must respect the warning signs. Humiliate yourself to the warning signs and heed them. This is not negotiable. There is no room for compromise.

While the addict could remain cocaine free fueled by the zeal of fools recovery and its inertia, it takes great heroic effort and a great mental battle to take on the myriad of challenges that will attack the body, emotions, will power and spirit.

Of paramount importance is rehabilitation. It alone comes first. First before all else. The addict must protect his sobriety before all else. Know that time will drop other things in place after great determination is given to remain drug free.

Inertia, propelled by forces other than direct efforts does work but is not reliable when sudden challenges arise that call on one to make decisions at the spur of the moment. Prayers and trust in God can be a major source of inertia. However, a person who refuses to obey basic recovery's does-and-don'ts is asking for trouble.

There is a thin line that exists between persons who stop drugs cold turkey and those that quit on inertia. A situation that can lead to cold turkey quitting is close encounter with death or simple conscience decision that there is no future in cocaine use. Some persons resolve go deep enough that their inner cry is heard by their spirits. They marshal the fortitude to conduct their lives then maneuver through the stumbling blocks.

There is a theory that persons who use clever ingenuity to maintain their addiction take a harder time quitting their habit. It is also assumed that persons of lesser ingenuity have the ability to just quit, and does not look back.

Coming out of structured rehabilitation, the key to survival is continued structure in your life. Let what works, work. The gaining of confidence is not a license for recklessness. Let what works, work.

The second month should be a repeat of the first. This life style could appear as dull and unchallenging. The longer the success strings along the more demanding the urges to use.

CHAPTER 15

LEAP OF FAITH THE BLIND, DARK JOURNEY

The addict must face his addiction, close his eyes, turn away from it then take that blind leap of faith by being lead through recovery. This is the hidden journey; the journey of darkness when all is let go then life on the other side realized.

Facing up to addiction head on and face to face then denying it plunging ones life into perceived unknowns naked without the crutches of that substance is like facing to jump from a high cliff. Such is the hold of addiction. However, that blind leap must come. Like being guided by angels the addict must allow life to take its wholesome embrace.

Closing one's eyes in the face of addiction then being lead away to a room of safety where the steps of recovery become those guiding and embracing angels must encompass the journey to recovery. Within the quiet of the soul found within that still, dark patch of faith the addict must gain the confidence of the blind who takes those first uncertain steps - but sure steps indeed.

Like the blind the journey will be wobbly at first and stumbles are a surety but one must not let go of the faith and somehow plow and plunge through the darkness of life. Within time strength and confidence will allow sure footing but know to walk up a cragged, rocky mountain will lead to light on the other side. The journey is a perilous must, but all addicts know the result of opening one's eyes then succumbing to the known painful chaotic forces that entrap and enslave the mind, body and soul in putrid bondage. It is a life we dare not venture again once we have reinvigorated the joy of cocaine and addiction recovery.

There is peace on the other side of the mountain. We just have to dream it.

CHAPTER 16

BIOFEEDBACK.

If a recovering addict were to place himself under biofeedback's ultimate test he will gain the knowledge of his inner emotional mechanisms. Unlike a timepiece's inner mechanisms, steady and methodical as its springs, our mechanisms tend to vary according shifting inner and external stimulations.

Imagine your skull and parts of your body with wires attached so as to monitor and register all brain activity and muscle twitches. A recovering addict could be at the bliss of relaxation at the flowery meadow and valley between two green mountains. With inner peace and tranquility all sensors to mind and body would read a steady straight line except for normal heart rate functions. Place a vile of cocaine within view of a recovering addict then all monitored points would explode to Mount Everest and appear as the jagged peaks of the Himalayan range.

At the sight or nuance of cocaine the meters will all go crazy like a Richter scale during a massive earthquake. However the earthquake this time is the massive mind and bodily reactions that surge out of control stimulated by cocaine. If a test could be developed to detect what happens to the spirit maybe tremors would rumble off the wall there also.

If an object, a book, clothing or anything non-stimulating to cocaine addiction is placed before the addict the meters would remain still. However, when cocaine or its paraphernalia are placed before an addict spontaneous and massive reactions take place. The mind and body assume an automatic out of control drive to obtain drugs then use it.

For non-addicts, the presence of cocaine or its paraphernalia would not cause a reaction. The addict could gauge his reactions to cocaine stimulations as a tool toward self-control and awareness through acquiring relaxation techniques from a trained psychiatric or yogic personnel.

Relaxation techniques deny the mind and body racing on that crashing runaway train; it keeps the mind and body in a state of tranquility where it is able to deny reacting to the cocaine crave and deflects all urges.

To gain bodily and mental still-conditions of absolute self control and tranquility necessary to maintain sobriety is crucial. Gaining mental control while in the face of agitation is absolute in order to remain drug free.

A recovering addict can never attain that non-responsive pre-addict stability in the face of exposure to cocaine. For the recovering addict the results would be instantaneously explosive as the heart rate accelerates to 300% - that must be subdued. Also breathing goes erratic, hot and passionate - that must be calmed. Muscles about the body stiffen then tense - that must calm to peacefulness.

Within minutes sweat beads at the forehead and under the armpits exude telltale, that the body and mind are raging wild and wanting. The eyes stare with narrow direct focused gaze toward the cocaine. The mind tunnels then narrows to that dungeon of enslaving pleasure that chases to corrupt and possess the whole being with all uncontrollable desires and evils that could possible ensue.

To close and control those mental and physical gates to anticipation that precipitate a sure cocaine use is paramount. Those gateways: the heart rate, cold sweat, dilated excited pupils, anxiety, irritation and tension must be forcefully and passionately mentally micromanaged and monitored. Having devises to ease then executing that mental kill-switch to shut down anticipation even though in the direct face of cocaine offers two options: to flee as a first course or to visualize by using relaxation techniques.

Relaxation and visualization redirect sights and thoughts to images of tranquility. These great imagery tools if utilized counter those uncontrollable tentacles, those jabs of anticipations that could paralyze the mind, body and soul toward cocaine use. Relaxation and forced imagery counter by suppressing cravings and the agitations to the mind and body by invoking calmness, control and peace.

During relaxation techniques each individual must have a dream haven where peace can be mentally realized through input imagery. For some it may be a beach scene, for others imagery of Mars tranquility. However done, from green grassy pearly gates, blue waters with white sand to the still and burnt desert emptiness of Mars, mind will overcome matter, calmness will ensue in the face of agitation.

Relaxations could begin by first shedding the stiff stress within the shoulders then the tension within the legs. Envelope the body as calmness flows across the body. Awareness having been made, you listen to your breathing then bring it to calm and still rhythms. Body brought into control the mind must be channeled into pre-practiced thoughts and imagery of tranquility. The rage of cocaine will cease.

ABOUT THE AUTHOR

Carlton Robinson is the author of COCAINE USE: THE ACCIDENT OF MY LIFE, Vantage Press 1989. The novel, HIGH: http://www.cocainehighsucks.com 1stbooks.com. Robinson has also published a series of short stories and poetry in his native Bahamas.

Robinson with twenty years cocaine free gives the inner perspective of recovery that ranges from addiction to compelling reasons to quit with relevant internal changes: months, a year, the magical six and then ten years clean.

A rich graph details a cocaine high from a sober state then the high phase to the suicidal effects of addiction. He takes one through the flux of conflict - decay and salvation - the inner core of self and peace, where recovery must first blossom.

Printed in the United States
153563LV00006B/90/A